//// NASCAR
CLASSICS

CLASSICS

BY THE AUTO EDITORS OF CONSUMER GUIDE®

Publications International, Ltd.

ISBN-13: 978-1-4508-2069-1
ISBN-10: 1-4508-2069-7

Manufactured in China.

8 7 6 5 4 3 2 1

Library of Congress Control Number: 2011920088

Credits

Photography:

The editors would like to thank the following people and organizations for supplying the photography that made this book possible. They are listed below, along with the page number(s) of their photos.

Ken Beebe: 117; **Chan Bush:** 83, 87; **Jack Cansler:** 14; **Greg Fielden:** 16, 52, 62, 88, 92, 104, 108, 120; **Alex Gabbard:** 55; **Bryan Hallman:** 122; **Jerry Heasley:** 59, 125; **Don Heiny:** 17; **International Speedway Corporation:** front cover, 10, 12, 18, 20, 22, 24, 26, 28, 32, 34, 40, 42, 46, 48, 50, 54, 56, 58, 60, 64, 66, 68, 70, 72, 74, 76, 78, 80, 82, 84, 86, 90, 94, 96, 98, 100, 102, 106, 112, 114, 116, 118, 124, 126, back cover; **Bud Juneau:** 93; **Tom Kirkland:** 30, 36, 38, 44; **Dan Lyons:** 73; **Vince Manocchi:** 15, 19, 29, 31, 35, 47, 71, 79, 99; **Doug Mitchel:** 9, 11, 41, 45, 51, 53, 57, 67, 69, 81, 95, 103; **Mike Mueller:** 21, 65; **Bob Nicholson:** 113; **William J. Schintz:** 97; **Richard Spiegelman:** 23; **David Temple:** 43, 61, 95, 111; **W. C. Waymack:** 11 (bottom middle), 13, 15 (bottom left), 25, 37, 39, 49, 77, 85, 105, 109; **Hub Wilson:** 33; **Nicky Wright:** 27; **Paul Zazarine:** 75

Owners:

Special thanks to the owners of the cars featured in this book for their cooperation. Their names and page numbers for their vehicles follow

Homer F. Altevogt: 37; **Art Astor:** 15; **Mark Auran:** 87; **Jim Bauldauf:** 11; **John A. Beekman:** 11; **Larry Bell:** 89; **Doug Bendle:** 55; **Brad Bishop:** 111; **Ken Block:** 29; **Gene Bowerbank:** 113; **Richard Carpenter:** 47; **Stanley and Phyllis Dumes:** 21; **John B. Garofal III:** 17; **Ed Giolma:** 61; **John Grieki Jr.:** 103; **William A. Harper:** 9; **Henry Hart:** 65; **Lloyd W. Hill:** 59; **Bill Hoff:** 125, back cover; **Richard Horner:** 75; **Lee Keeney:** 77; **John and Minnie Keys:** 19; **James Kwiatkowski:** 81; **George Lux:** 79, back cover; **Guy Mabee:** 69; **Dan Mamsen:** 63; **Larry Martin:** 109; **Bill May:** 43; **John and Vicki Mayer:** 45; **Greg and Rhonda Meredyk:** 71; **Larry and Karen Miller:** 117; **Glenn Moist:** 51; **Richard Monaco:** 67; **Bob Moore:** 41; **Phil Newcomb:** 99; **E. M. Pascarella:** 57; **Glen and Janice Pykiet:** 39; **David Ramaly:** 95; **Ramshead Automobile Collection:** 93; **Larry and Annis Ray:** 31; **Jim & Sharron Reid:** 23; **Gary Richards:** 35; **Dennis D. Rosenberry:** 97, back cover; **Otto T. Rosenbusch:** 27; **Ardie and Doris Sabo:** 13; **Steve Smith:** 49; **Thomas J. Sory:** 85; **Michael Tesauro:** 73; **Dick Towers:** 87; **Bill Ulrich:** 33; **Ron Voyes:** 91; **Donald Walkenmeyer:** 25, back cover; **Dave and Norma Wasilewski:** 53; **Leroy and Judy Williams:** 105.

CONTENTS

INTRODUCTION

Almost as long as there have been cars, there have been manufacturers that competed against each other in racing. But at no previous time was the competition so fierce and the reward for winning so great as after the birth of the racing association known as NASCAR.

Prior to 1950, most of the grass-roots auto racing in the U.S. involved independent drivers running "modifieds"; production cars that were stripped-down and hopped-up until the make and model became difficult to identify. That began to change when the year-old NASCAR organization ran its first Strictly Stock race between showroom-stock automobiles on June 19, 1949. The contest proved so popular with fans that more "stock car" races were quickly added to the schedule, and the NASCAR series soon became a national phenomenon.

What really got the ball rolling, however, was the recognition by auto manufacturers that victories on the track translated into sales in the showroom. This "Win on Sunday, Sell on Monday" philosophy caused the Big Three and even some of the independent makes to take an active roll in racing, both by supporting teams and creating ever-more-powerful cars. The latter spurred the "Horsepower race" of the 1950s that reached its zenith in the early '70s.

Although the original intent was to run showroom-stock cars—and strict rules were instituted to ensure that—it wasn't long before safety-related modifications were mandated. Gradually, more and more under-skin changes were allowed, but well into the 1970s, the cars essentially remained modified production vehicles. Even after specialized chassis were sanctioned in the early '80s, the cars still looked like their counterparts in the showroom. It wasn't until Detroit began a seismic shift to front-wheel drive and V-6 engines in the mid-'80s that the race cars became mechanically divorced from those on the street, yet the bodies still bore more than a passing resemblance. *NASCAR Classics* celebrates the cars—and the competition—that helped the organization through its formative years and on to the success it enjoys today.

1949
Lincoln

Lincolns boasted a sleek redesign for 1949, with smooth-fendered "bathtub" styling replacing the boxier, separate-fender look of the '48s. Also new—and infinitely more important to race car drivers—was a 152-horsepower 337-cubic-inch flathead V-8 that supplanted a 125-hp flathead V-12. Lincolns were offered in two sizes for 1949: a lower-cost 121-inch-wheelbase version that shared its basic bodyshell with that year's Mercury, and the 125-inch-wheelbase Cosmopolitan. A short-wheelbase coupe was the lightest car in the lineup, tipping the scales at a hair less than two tons. But that mass was offset by the big V-8's power, and Lincolns managed to win two

NASCAR events in 1949. The first was of particular significance: It was the inaugural NASCAR Strictly Stock race, a new series that quickly became the primary NASCAR drawing card. Unlike Modifieds, NASCAR Strictly Stock cars had to be just that: strictly stock. Lincolns may have won more races if they hadn't been so expensive. Drivers were typically on a tight budget, and, at $2527, the cheapest Lincoln cost a grand more than a Ford V-8. Thus a base Lincoln coupe, like the blue car shown at right, was sort of a "Gentleman's racer," which—win or lose—made for a nice ride home from the track.

Ken Wagner's Lincoln leads a pair of Oldsmobiles and a Cadillac in the 1949 NASCAR Strictly Stock season finale at North Wilkesboro Speedway in North Carolina. The Lincoln was the fastest qualifier at an average speed of 57.563 mph, but retired midway through the race with mechanical problems.

1949
Oldsmobile 88

When Oldsmobile introduced its modern overhead-valve "Rocket V-8" for 1949, the company probably didn't know it would be powering the first "superstar" of NASCAR. And that probably wouldn't have been the case if Olds had stuck to the usual plan of putting the biggest engine only in the biggest car. Instead, the company applied what would later be called the "muscle-car formula" by offering its potent V-8 in the lighter, entry-level 88 model (a yellow convertible is shown at right) rather than in just the larger, heavier 98. The rest is history. Oldsmobiles won five of eight NASCAR Strictly Stock races in 1949, 10 of 19 the following year, and 20 of 41 in 1951. Initially rated at 130 horsepower, the 303-cubic-inch overhead-valve V-8 wasn't the strongest powerplant of the late 1940s, but it powered a club coupe (a blue, six-cylinder, Series 76 club coupe is shown at right) that weighed 3550 lbs.—significantly less than a more-powerful Lincoln or Cadillac. Furthermore, a race car driver could buy one for $2143, making it significantly less expensive as well. The fact that the '49 Olds carried sleek new styling was probably of less concern on track than off, but certainly didn't hurt the car's popularity.

Red Byron in the #22 Oldsmobile heads down the frontstretch at Charlotte Speedway in North Carolina during the first-ever NASCAR Strictly Stock race on June 19, 1949. Byron didn't win this event, but he would pilot his Olds to two victories that year—and the NASCAR championship.

1950
Plymouth

If ever there were unlikely "star cars of NASCAR," they would be the early-'50s Plymouths. Receiving their first postwar redesign midway through the 1949 model year, Chrysler Corporation's price leaders continued their tradition of what might charitably be called "conservative" styling. Equally conservative was the engine: a 217-cubic-inch flathead six that dated back to a 201-cid version introduced for 1933. Strangely, however, the engine was rated at 97 horsepower by this time, five more than Chevrolet's more advanced overhead-valve six of virtually the same displacement.

Plymouths also weighed about 150 pounds less than comparable Chevys, so they had a fairly good power-to-weight ratio for a low-priced car. Perhaps it shouldn't be too surprising then that these rather stodgy Plymouths managed nine wins from 1950 through 1952, more than any make besides Hudson and Oldsmobile. Most noteworthy was a victory in the inaugural Southern 500 in 1950. The race was run at the new Darlington Raceway in Darlington, South Carolina, the first superspeedway to host a NASCAR event.

Lee Petty's #42 Plymouth leans mightily into a turn during a 1950 race at Martinsville Speedway in Martinsville, Virginia. Petty took third in the event and wound up third in the standings. Petty scored more points during the year than any other driver but was docked more than half of them after entering a non-NASCAR event midway through the season.

1951
Chrysler Saratoga

"That thing got a Hemi?" Although the expression wouldn't become popular until decades later, the first time someone could answer "You bet!" was when driving a 1951 Chrysler. The company introduced one of America's most famous engines that year as a 331-cubic-inch beast that produced an industry-leading 180 horsepower. Compared with the relatively tidy-looking Cadillac and Oldsmobile overhead-valve V-8s, the Hemi had canted valves resulting in huge heads that nearly filled the Chrysler's sizable engine bay from fenderwell to fenderwell. The entry-level Chrysler was the six-cylinder Windsor that started at

$2368 (a yellow Windsor Newport hardtop coupe is shown at right), but the cheapest car to offer the Hemi (opposite page, bottom left) was the very similar $2989, 3948-pound Saratoga club coupe, which made it too pricey for most drivers. Perhaps as a result, Chrysler was victorious in just a single event that year, but it was a big one: the Motor City 250 at Detroit's Michigan State Fairgrounds, the first to bring a NASCAR event to the doorstep of the Big Three. As such, it stirred up manufacturer interest and support of NASCAR racing, which is hugely responsible for building the sport into what it is today.

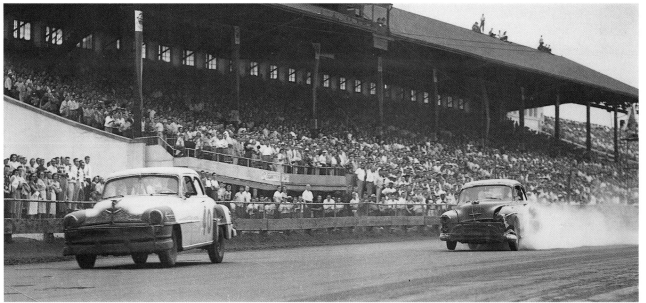

The inaugural Motor City 250 turned out to be one of the most thrilling races in NASCAR history. Newcomer Tommy Thompson, driving the #40 Chrysler, locked horns with hard-charging veteran Curtis Turner in the final laps. As they dueled for the lead, the Chrysler and Turner's Oldsmobile collided in the third turn. As they zoomed down the front chute, Turner's mangled Olds started to smoke, leaving Thompson to take the victory. Partly because it was run in front of Detroit automotive executives, 15 different makes of cars entered the race.

1951
Studebaker Commander

In the early years of NASCAR Strictly Stock competition, the powerful Oldsmobiles and Hudsons were clearly the cars of choice. Yet other makes made their mark, partly because the race did not always go to the swift. Independently owned Studebaker didn't have the recognition or sales clout of the Big Three, but the company made some interesting cars in the early postwar years. In 1947, the company became one of the first to roll out all-new postwar models when the Big Three were still churning out warmed-over prewar cars. These were updated with "bullet-nose" styling for 1950, though engines remained the same: straight sixes of 170 cubic inches for Champions, 245 cid for top-line Commanders. But for 1951, Studebaker introduced a new 232-cid V-8 for Commanders that put out 120 horsepower vs. 102 from the six, and the cars became uncharacteristically quick. Whether this move was at all prompted by a quest for racing victories is unclear, but it did result in a brief glimmer of success on the NASCAR circuit. All of that "brief glimmer" came in 1951, when Studebakers won its first and last NASCAR race, with one in between.

Having qualified second fastest, Frank Mundy's #23 Studebaker sits on the outside of the first row next to pole-sitter Herb Thomas at Jacksonville. Thomas went on to win while Mundy came in fifth. Mundy earned four poles and two victories in his Studebaker during the season, and finished an impressive fifth in the points standings.

1952
Hudson Hornet

Hudson wasn't really known for performance when it introduced the famous Step-Down models for 1948. While most cars of the era had their floorpan mounted above the frame rails, the Step-Down design carried it below the frame rails. Not only did this bring better passenger protection, it also resulted in a lower center of gravity—and thus, better handling. Also new that year was a larger flathead inline six-cylinder engine, though the line's available flathead inline eight carried over unchanged. Neither made enough power to give Hudsons an edge on the race track. But that changed for 1951. Introduced that year was a huge 308-cubic-inch flathead six producing 145 horsepower—more than Oldsmobile's contemporary 303-cid overhead-valve V8. The engine went into a new model called the Hornet, and its combination of relatively light weight, terrific handling, and strong engine made it the new star of NASCAR racing. The star burned even brighter for 1953, when the Hornet's base six was pushed to 160 hp, and a new twin-carb 7-X version made 170. Hudsons won 66 of 112 NASCAR Strictly Stock events from 1952 to 1954, and the Manufacturers Championship (started in 1952) each of those years.

Tim Flock in his Hudson Hornet slightly trails brother Fonty in an Oldsmobile as the two lead the charge down the straightaway at Occoneechee Speedway in Hillsborough, North Carolina. However, Tim was ahead when the checkered flag dropped, giving Hudson one of its 27 wins of the 34-race 1952 NASCAR season.

1953
Dodge Coronet

When Chrysler introduced its 331-cubic-inch Hemi V-8 in 1951, it turned the company's Saratoga into a production hot rod. Two years later, a smaller version of the engine did the same for the Dodge Coronet. Previously offered only with inline sixes, Dodges were considered slightly upscale of Chevrolets and Fords but hardly upscale in performance. That changed when the redesigned 1953 line debuted carrying the new Hemi-powered Coronet Eight. Advertised as the "Red Ram V-8," Dodge's Hemi displaced 241 cubic inches and produced 140 horsepower—healthy for the day—and the lightest Coronet Eight it powered weighed just over 3300 pounds. As such, the car's power-to-weight ratio gave it impressive performance, and prices starting at less than $2200 made it attractive to race car drivers. (At the time, the cheapest Hudson Hornet cost $2742.) Not surprisingly, Dodge recorded its first NASCAR victory in 1953—and then went on to take five more. Only Hudson (22 wins) and Oldsmobile (with nine) did better that year.

A 1953 Dodge Coronet runs just inside the #54 Hudson of Obie Chupp as the cars round the south turn of the famed 4.15-mile Daytona Beach & Road Course in Daytona Beach, Florida. Although he didn't compete in this race, Lee Petty, father of Richard Petty, drove Dodges to five wins in 1953 and finished second in the points standings.

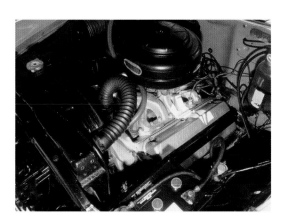

1954

Oldsmobile 88

Although the company's early NASCAR glory days were brought to an end by the Hudson Hornet, Oldsmobile continued to be competitive through the 1950s. In fact, one of the make's best seasons was in 1954, when Oldsmobiles won 11 races. The lineup was redesigned that year with modern, "straight-through" styling that completely erased any hint of separate rear fenders and brought with it an enlarged V-8 bumped from 303 cubic inches to 324. The new engine produced up to 185 horsepower, once again making Oldsmobile a car to contend with on the track. Prices started at $2272 for a 170-hp 88 two-door sedan, but race car drivers often opted for the $2410 Super 88 version with the 185-hp V-8. (A $2688 Super 88 Deluxe Holiday hardtop coupe is shown at right.) Tim Flock drove the #88 Olds that recorded a "first" in the NASCAR record books. It was equipped with a General Electric two-way radio that allowed Flock to speak with his pit crew during the race, a major innovation for the day.

Tim Flock in the #88 Oldsmobile rounds the north turn of the Daytona Beach & Road Course in 1954. Flock took the checkered flag, but not the trophy. During the post-race inspection, it was found that the carburetor in Flock's Olds had been modified—a violation of the rules—and his car was disqualified.

1955
Chevrolet

In the early days of NASCAR, Chevrolets had long been big winners in the sales race, but they were never big winners on the track. In fact, through the 1954 season, the make had amassed a grand total of... zero victories. Among its direct showroom rivals, Ford had scored a win, Studebaker had three, and Plymouth had ten. But that all changed in 1955 when Chevrolets were redesigned with modern styling that would later render them classics. More important to the make's NASCAR hopes, however, was the introduction of the famed "small-block Chevy V-8." Originally sized at 265 cubic inches, the thoroughly

modern overhead-valve V-8 put out up to 180 horse-power, whereas the top previous engine—a 235-cid inline six—couldn't muster more than 125. While the new Bel Air was the flashy '55 Chevy, race car drivers typically went with the budget One-Fifty series, though some sprung for the midline Two-Ten shown at right. In any event, the combination of the new V-8, curb weights that hovered around 3100 pounds, and prices well under $2000 made Chevys more popular at the tracks, and the make scored its first two wins in 1955. Of course, the car was also quite popular in the showroom, but that's an entirely different story.

Early in the 1955 season, Fonty Flock raced the #14 Chevrolet, driving it to the make's first NASCAR victory in March of that year at Columbia Speedway in Columbia, South Carolina. Race cars of this era were essentially stock, with many drivers taking a "run what you brung" attitude ... and apparently the Buick driver trailing Flock hadn't "brung" any door numbers.

1955
Chrysler 300

Although numerous manufacturers brought out potent new engines for 1955, Chrysler stayed ahead of the pack with a special "tuned" version of its famous 331-cubic-inch Hemi V-8. It was offered only in a new sport-luxury model called the 300, which took its name from the 300 horses it corralled. (Other Chryslers with that same basic engine had "only" 250 horsepower.) The 300 came only as a flashy hardtop coupe with a list price of $4110—solidly in Cadillac territory. As such, it was out of reach for most NASCAR drivers. It wasn't out of reach, however, for Carl Kiekhaefer. Kiekhaefer was head of Mercury

Outboard, a builder of outboard motors for boats, and he bought a fleet of 300s and started a team that included some of the top drivers in NASCAR. For the 1955 running of the famed Daytona Beach race, Kiekhaefer fielded a team of six Chrysler 300s, the one driven by Tim Flock taking the checkered flag. It marked the first appearance for the team and the first of 22 wins for the season. Whether any of that mattered to the 1725 well-heeled souls who managed to buy a 300 that year is unclear. What is not in doubt is the unrivaled success of the car in competition and its esteemed place in the minds of collectors today.

Tim Flock in the aptly numbered 300 Chrysler 300 leads his brother and teammate Fonty Flock in a close-quarters battle at Martinsville Speedway in Martinsville, Virginia. Tim went on to win the race, one of 18 victories that year that helped him secure the Drivers Championship.

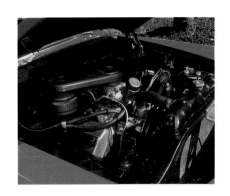

1956
Chrysler 300-B

By mid-1956, it was becoming an increasingly common sight: one of team owner Carl Kiekhaefer's big white Chryslers once again leading a race—frequently from start to finish. After winning an impressive 22 races in 1955, he topped that mark in '56 with 30 victories, including 16 in a row between March and June. Helping him in his cause was Chrysler's update of its sport-luxury 300 model, renamed 300-B for 1956. The transformation to a "letter-series" car (actually, modern collectors consider the original 300 as one of them) brought an even larger, more-powerful version of the Hemi, growing from 331 cubic inches and 300 horsepower to 354 cid and 355 hp. As such, it became the first production engine to reach the magic "one horsepower per cubic inch" mark. Styling was altered with a revised grille and larger tailfins, but Chrysler's top-line model was still available only as a hardtop coupe. The price shot up to $4419, which didn't seem to faze Kiekhaefer—or about 1100 other buyers. He pulled out of racing at the end of the '56 season, but for his considerable efforts—and expense—Kiekhaefer set numerous NASCAR records that will likely never be broken.

Tim Flock in the number 300-A Chrysler 300-B leads a pack through the north turn in the early laps of the February 26, 1956, Daytona Beach NASCAR race. Flock went on to win the event, leading all 37 laps on the 4.15-mile Beach & Road Course. Flock's car was owned and prepared by the powerful Kiekhaefer team, which won 30 of the 51 events it entered that year.

1956

Ford

Despite Ford's early success in NASCAR's Modified division with prewar flathead V-8s, the company hadn't been faring well on the race tracks in the Fifties. Even a switch to a modern overhead-valve V-8 for 1954 didn't do much good, partly because—at 239 cubic inches—it just wasn't very big. The V-8 was enlarged for 1955 into 272- and 292-cid versions, producing up to 182 and 198 horsepower, respectively, and that change was enough to finally bring Ford a pair of victories. But the Blue Oval was just getting started. Another bump in displacement for '56 brought a 312-cid engine with up to 225 hp, and with

that, Ford went on a tear. Not only did the company's cars win 14 races that year, but they also gave Ford the Manufacturers Championship. One of Ford's strategies that made the cars popular with NASCAR drivers was that the strongest engine was available in all models in the line, including the price-leading Mainline and mid-level Customline, which started well under $2000. Furthermore, Ford added a recessed steering-wheel hub and optional padded dash for safety. The fact that it was also a very good-looking car didn't hurt, either, as the '56s wore a sleek update of the redesigned-for-'55 body shell.

Curtis Turner flashes down the front chute in his #99 Ford while taking the checkered flag at the Southern 500. It proved to be his only victory of the season, but it was a big one. Held at Darlington Raceway in Darlington, South Carolina, the Southern 500 was one of the premier races on the NASCAR schedule.

1957
Chevrolet

It has since become the poster child of 1950s Americana, but in its day, the '57 Chevy was just a third-year update to the 1955 bodyshell. Significantly, it came in second to Ford in sales, only the fourth time that had happened since the end of World War II. It was the same story on the tracks. Chevys won an impressive 21 races, but Fords won an even more-impressive 26. Both makes became increasingly popular with drivers due to the fact that in 1957, the Automobile Manufacturers Association (AMA) announced that factory support of racing would be suspended due to fears that speeds on the track were adversely affecting safety on the streets. With manufacturer support (read "dollars") gone, teams had to look for less-expensive cars, and Chevy was happy to oblige, offering an entry-level One-Fifty with V-8 (shown at right) for less than $2000. Those with deeper pockets could opt for the top engine, a fuel-injected 283-cubic-inch V-8 producing up to 283 horsepower (shown top right). However, NASCAR soon banned fuel injection and supercharging. Although some drivers chose to race mid-line Two-Ten models, top-line Bel Airs were rarely seen on the track.

Buck Baker in the #87 Chevy leads Jack Smith in the #47 Chevy as they pass the #154 Ford of Nace Mattingly at the Wilson Speedway in Wilson, North Carolina. Baker finished second in this race but won 10 others during the season along with the Drivers Championship at the end.

1957

Ford

A combination of the 1957 AMA ban on factory support of racing and the fact that even some of Detroit's less-expensive makes were deeply immersed in the horsepower race (which, some might add, was at least partially responsible for the AMA ban in the first place) drove many teams to shift their automotive allegiances to Chevy and Ford for the 1957 NASCAR season. As a result, the two makes combined for 47 wins in the 53-race schedule, the only other manufacturers taking victories being Oldsmobile (four) and Pontiac (two). Ford edged out Chevy with 26 wins and earned the Manufacturers Championship for the second year in a row. Ford was also victorious in the showrooms. Offering redesigned cars against Chevy's facelifted ones (albeit a handsome facelift, indeed), Fords looked more modern and had power to back up the pomp. Displacements stayed the same, but the top 312-cubic-inch V-8 was boosted from 215 horsepower to 245, and as before, was offered in all trim levels. Some names were new: The base model was now the Custom (shown at right), then came the Custom 300, the returning Fairlane, and a new top-line model, the Fairlane 500. Ford sold a bunch of the upper-series cars, but these were rarely raced.

The #99 Ford of Curtis Turner slides through the north turn of the Daytona Beach & Road Course. Turner finished seventh, and the highest-ranking Ford came in fifth, making Daytona one of just two races of the season in which a Ford didn't finish in the top four. It was also one of only two races that year won by a Pontiac.

1958
Chevrolet

Chevrolet's 1958 full-size line was fully redesigned with styling that was a complete departure from the '57 look. Shorn of traditional tailfins, it had detailed bodyside sculpting and four headlights, the latter being newly legal in all states. Some model names were also changed, the lineup starting with the Delray, then moving up through Biscayne to the returning Bel Air shown at right. Debuting the Impala moniker were top-trim hardtop coupes and convertibles with either six-cylinder or V-8 power. Chevy bested Ford this year both on track and off, winning 25 of 51 NASCAR races, the Manufactuers Championship, and the "USA-1" sales crown. But only the last can be credited to the 1958 models. Due to the 1957 AMA ban

that "discouraged" factories from supporting racing activities, most teams that had '57 Chevys continued to run them on the tracks the following year. Some teams, however, spent the money on a new '58 Chevy. Although larger and heavier than the '57s, the '58 offered a new, top engine: a truck-based "big-block" V-8 of 348 cubic inches producing from 250 to 315 horsepower. Still offered were a 145-hp 235-cid six and 283-cid "small-block" V-8s ranging from 185 to 290 hp. Despite its obvious appeal—and contrary to Chevy's usual strategy—the '58 body style lasted only one year; it was replaced for '59 by another complete redesign that once again looked nothing like its predecessor.

A number of Chevrolets scored victories during the 1958 NASCAR season, but this wasn't one of them. Rookie driver Don Kimberling in the #60 Chevrolet spun his car in front of George Dunn in the #14 Mercury in the early laps of the Southern 500 at Darlington in Kimberling's first—and last—NASCAR race.

1958
Ford

Although Chevrolet won more NASCAR races and the sales crown in 1958, Ford was a close second in both. However, the two makes did have one thing in common: most of their cars seen on NASCAR tracks that year were 1957 models. This was largely the result of financial cutbacks required when manufacturer support dried up due to the AMA's racing ban, and most teams that had factory cars in 1957 were allowed to keep them. Still, some teams sprung for a new '58 Ford—and for good reason. It wasn't because the company's full-size line was facelifted that year with quad headlights and four oblong taillamps; it was more likely due to the fact that Ford offered two enlarged V-8s to replace the former top-line 312-cubic incher: a 332-cid version offering 240-265 horsepower, and a 352 with 300 hp. Model choices included Custom and Custom 300 on a 116-inch wheelbase, and Fairlane and Fairlane 500 (shown at right) on a 118-inch span. It's likely most NASCAR drivers who raced a '58 Ford chose one of the shorter, lighter cars with the biggest engine, as many boasted "300 H.P." on their hoods.

Joe Weatherly's #12 Ford leads the #45 Ford of Eddie Pagan into the first turn at Darlington during the Southern 500. Trailing in this photo is the #26 Ford of Curtis Turner. All these Fords are 1958 models, but '57 Fords were probably more numerous overall during the season. Right behind Pagan is Fireball Roberts, who drove his #22 1957 Chevrolet to victory, and the #6 Pontiac of Joe Eubanks.

1959
Chevrolet

Although Chevrolet's full-size line had been redesigned for 1958, it got another complete makeover for '59. Most notable were the large "eyebrows" over the headlights and distinct "batwing" horizontal tailfins. Rooflines were new, with dogleg front pillars and thin, swept-back rear pillars except on the Sport Sedan, which had a flat-top roof and near-vertical rear pillars. Topping the engine chart was the same truck-based, 348-cubic-inch big-block V-8 introduced for 1958, still with up to 315 horsepower. A 235-cid six and a slew of 283-cid V-8s were also available. Biscayne was

now the entry-level model, followed by Bel Air; most NASCAR teams chose one or the other, as the 348 was offered in both. The Impala nameplate, introduced on top-line coupes and convertibles for '58, now offered a wide selection of body styles, including the Sport hardtop coupe shown at right. Chevrolet and Ford tied with 16 NASCAR wins each, but Chevy took the Manufacturers Championship. Note, however, that most of Ford's victories were earned by either 1957 models or '59 Thunderbirds, not the company's regular full-size cars.

The famed Daytona International Speedway opened its gates in 1959 and hosted the inaugural Daytona 500 that year. In one of the more courageous acts of the event, Johnny Bruner Sr. flagged off the start from the apron of the track as pole-sitter Bob Welborn blew by in his '59 Chevy barely five feet away.

1959
Ford Thunderbird

NASCAR record books show that Ford was credited with 16 wins during the 1959 season, but the vast majority were scored by either 1957 models or '59 Thunderbirds rather than members of the company's regular full-size line. Thunderbirds became eligible for NASCAR competition after switching from a two-seat design to a four-passenger body in 1958. Compared with most competing cars—such as the '59 Chevrolet and Plymouth—the T-Bird was smaller but also heavier, nearly the weight of the big Oldsmobiles. However, this was more than offset by a new-for-'59 430-cubic-inch V-8 rated at 350 horsepower, an engine that was significantly larger and more powerful than even that in the Olds. As such, the "Squarebirds" had a great power-to-weight ratio, enough to overcome any aerodynamic disadvantage afforded by their rather blocky styling. During Daytona Speedweeks—the car's first NASCAR appearance—T-Birds came in second in both the 100-mile qualifying race and the Daytona 500, the latter by a mere whisker. They accounted for six of Ford's 16 victories, a tremendous achievement in a car's first year of racing.

It turned out to be a literal photo finish in the first Daytona 500 as Johnny Beauchamp in the #73 Thunderbird and Lee Petty in the #42 Oldsmobile appeared to cross the finish line in a dead heat. Running on the outside was Joe Weatherly, who was two laps down and thus not in contention. Although Beauchamp was initially thought to have won, photographs and film footage showed Petty to be the victor.

1959
Oldsmobile

Oldsmobile maintained a steady stream of NASCAR victories during the 1950s, racking up at least one every year and a total of 79 during the decade. However, that string was about to come to an end; after winning four races in 1959, the make wouldn't take another checkered flag until the late '70s. But what a way to bow out. At the inaugural running of the Daytona 500, Lee Petty in a '59 Olds edged out Johnny Beauchamp in a Thunderbird to take the victory in what has since become the premier event on the NASCAR calendar. Oldsmobile itself had been regularly finishing fourth or fifth in the sales race during the late '50s, at least partially on the strength of a continued performance image and cars that looked decidedly different every year. For 1959, the make adopted jet-age styling with minimal tailfins along with airy greenhouses and thin-pillar rooflines. Horsepower had been steadily increasing, with up to 315 offered for '59 from the top V-8 that had been enlarged that year from 371 to 394 cubic inches. The model line included the base Dynamic 88, midline Super 88, and larger Ninety-Eight. Only the last two offered the 394-cid V-8, so the hot rod of the line was the Super 88 shown at right.

Lee Petty in the #42 Oldsmobile leads Johnny Beauchamp in the #73 Thunderbird in the closing laps of the inaugural Daytona 500. Running the high groove in the #48 Chevrolet is Joe Weatherly, who was two laps down. In the end, Petty and Beauchamp crossed the finish line neck-and-neck, with Beauchamp proclaimed the unofficial winner. But after 61 hours of studying photographs and film footage, the decision was reversed, and Petty was credited with the victory.

1959
Plymouth

Until 1959, Plymouth had a rather odd NASCAR history. Its extremely plebeian early-'50s six-cylinder cars managed to win a surprising number of races (nine from 1950 to 1952), but then the make entered a dry spell despite the introduction of a V-8 for 1955. That changed when, in mid-1959, the strong Petty Engineering team—which now included both father Lee and son Richard—switched from Oldmobiles to Plymouths, and Lee racked up seven late-season wins for the make. Plymouths of the era boasted

Chysler's "Forward Look," with the tallest tailfins in the low-priced field. For 1959, styling was updated with even taller fins, a garish eggcrate grill, and headlights topped by "siamesed" eyelids. The line included the base Savoy, midline Belvedere, and top Fury and Sport Fury (the convertible shown at right), all offered with up to 305 horsepower from a newly enlarged 361-cubic-inch V-8. Most 1959 buyers—among them, the Pettys—chose the base Savoy, at least in part due to a national recession that had hit the year before.

A special match race was run at the Orange Speedway in Hillsborough, North Carolina, between the father-son teams of Lee and Richard Petty and Buck and Buddy Baker. Richard Petty started on the pole in his '59 Plymouth, but Buddy Baker won the race in his Thunderbird.

1960
Chevrolet

Chevrolets were facelifted for 1960 but retained their horizontal tailfins, now positioned above individual round taillights—the latter a theme that would carry the make nearly to the end of the decade. Meanwhile, front ends got a cleaner look devoid of '59's nostrils. A 235-cubic-inch six returned as the base engine, with a 283-cid small-block being standard on V-8 models. A 348-cubic-inch V-8 returned as the top under-hood choice. It was now rated at up to 335 horsepower, 20 more than the previous year, though NASCAR teams used a 320-hp version as indicated

by the numbers on their cars' hoods. While this made them look like 98-pound weaklings next to the 360-hp Fords, Chevy took the Manufacturers Championship for the third year in a row, despite winning only 13 races to Ford's 15. The lineup was a virtual rerun from '59, though a Biscayne Fleetmaster—which slightly undercut the price of the low-line Biscayne—was added. The Biscayne was far outsold by the mid-line Bel Air (shown at right), yet the best seller was the top-line Impala.

Rex White in the #4 Chevrolet battles Glen Wood in the #21 Ford at Martinsville's ½-mile track during the Old Dominion 500. White finished fourth in this contest, but his Chevrolet netted him six wins for the season along with the Drivers Championship.

1960
Ford

During the 1958 and '59 NASCAR seasons, nearly all Ford victories were scored by either 1957 full-size models or 1959 Thunderbirds. The former were no longer eligible in 1960 (although they raced in the first two events of the season, which were held in November 1959), but were ably replaced by Ford's redesigned 1960 full-size models. Featuring horizontal tailfins that seemed to mimic those of the '59 Chevrolet, these cars were significantly longer, lower, and wider than their predecessors, something that didn't help curb weights any. But any increase in heft was more than made up for by a leap in horsepower. Although the 352-cubic-inch V-8 introduced for 1958 still hadn't grown by 1960, it packed a much bigger punch: up from 300 horsepower in 1959 to a whopping 360 hp for 1960. Fords competing in NASCAR proclaimed that loudly on their hoods, making 305-hp Plymouths, 320-hp Chevys, and 333-hp Pontiacs look like second-string players by comparison. Still, Ford came up second in points for both the Manufacturers Championship and the showroom sales race, once again losing the top spots to Chevrolet.

Joe Weatherly in the #12 Ford leads Rex White in the #4 Chevy into the first turn at Martinsville Speedway in Virginia during the Old Dominion 500. While White eventually won this battle—and the 1960 Drivers Championship—Weatherly would go on to win his share of races, along with the Drivers Championship in 1962 and '63.

1960
Plymouth

As had been the case in 1959, Plymouth owed its 1960 NASCAR success to the father-son team of Lee and Richard Petty. Richard scored his first three NASCAR wins that year while Lee added five more, the pair being solely responsible for Plymouth's eight victories. While Richard's first win came at the wheel of a 1959 Plymouth, all other victories by the Petty team were in 1960 models, which stood out by virtue of their tall, sharply protruding tailfins. Ever since its introduction in 1955, Plymouth's top V-8 had grown in displacement every year and, by 1960, was

pegged at 383 cubic inches with 330 horsepower. That engine wasn't eligible for NASCAR, however, as it featured two four-barrel carburetors on a cross-ram manifold. As a result, the Pettys had to "make do" with a 361-cid version topped by a single four-barrel good for 305 hp. Despite rather odd styling (which maybe didn't seem so in 1960), Plymouth maintained its traditional third-place finish behind Chevrolet and Ford in the sales race, a position it would soon forfeit—and not see again until the Seventies.

Lee Petty leads team-mate Bobby Johns in the inaugural running of the World 600 at Charlotte Motor Speedway in North Carolina. Richard Petty is in the seventh car back. The Petty team finished third, fourth, and fifth, but Lee and Richard were both disqualified for making "improper" entrances to the pits.

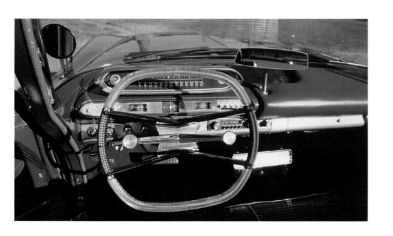

1960
Pontiac

Pontiac had long been known for solid but rather stodgy cars positioned one step above Chevrolet on the GM corporate ladder. Even after replacing its aged flathead straight sixes and eights with a modern overhead-valve V-8 for 1955, Pontiac didn't make much of a performance splash, and it wasn't until 1957 that the company scored its first NASCAR victory. Through the end of the decade, the make managed to rack up six wins, still not a stellar achievement. But in 1960, Pontiac more than doubled its victory count in a single year, taking the checkered flag in seven events. That marked the beginning of a brief but glorious NASCAR presence for the brand

that really started with the "Wide-Track Pontiac" of 1959, which lived up to its billing with a track that was nearly five inches wider than before. By 1960, that same platform was hosting a 389-cubic-inch V-8 boasting up to 348 horsepower with "Tri-Power" (triple two-barrel) carburetion, but the top engine eligible for NASCAR was a version with a single four-barrel carb rated at 333 hp—the figure shown on the cars' hoods. The model lineup included Catalina and Ventura on a shorter wheelbase than the higher-line Star Chief and Bonneville, and as might be expected, most teams raced the shorter, lighter, cheaper models, such as the Ventura pictured at right.

A trio of 1960 Pontiacs take the pace lap with a '59 Pontiac during the 1960 Daytona Speedweeks. Driving the #22 Pontiac (inside of second row) is Fireball Roberts, who set the fastest qualifying speed at more than 151 mph. Ahead of him in the #6 Pontiac is Cotton Owens, who won the pole-position race. Beside Owens in the #47 Pontiac is Jack Smith, who won a 100-mile preliminary race. None fared well in the Daytona 500, however. Roberts blew his engine, Owens lunched his transmission and Smith finished 23rd.

1961
Chevrolet

Chevrolets were redesigned for 1961 with smooth lines devoid of tailfins. The cars were slightly down-sized—losing about 70 pounds—and could easily be identified from the rear by a V-shaped trim line that bisected the taillight panel. That panel held two lamps on each side for the Biscayne and mid-line Bel Air, three for the top-line Impala shown at right. Most engine choices remained the same, though the 348-cubic-inch big-block V-8 now put out up to 350 horsepower. That, however, was not the Big Dog for 1961. Added to the options list that year was an even bigger big-block, the soon-to-be-famous 409. It put out 360 hp, which was broadcast on Chevrolet hoods in NASCAR competition. Although Pontiac easily topped the win column in 1961 with 30 victories out of 51 races, Chevrolet's tally of 11 wins helped it earn the Manufacturers Championship for the fourth year in a row.

Defending NASCAR champ Rex White, in the #4 Chevrolet, passes Tim Flock's #83 Ford in the early laps of the Daytona 500. White went on to finish 12th in his self-owned Chevy and just missed winning the Drivers Championship in '61. Ned Jarrett, driving a factory-sponsored Chevrolet, edged out White for the title.

1961
Plymouth

Described by one wag as looking like "The bug that ate Tokyo," the 1961 Plymouth's restyled front end could perhaps be more charitably called "distinctive." Combined with a tail treatment that sheared off the previous gigantic fins, the car looked nothing like its showroom predecessor, a potential contribution to the make's sales-position drop from its traditional third-place finish (behind Chevrolet and Ford) to fourth (passed by Rambler). But the slide was almost certainly not the result of lacking available power. Added above the previous 330-horsepower 383-

cubic-inch V-8 was a new 413-cid version with up to 375 hp. This engine was available in the base Savoy and mid-line Belvedere (the latter shown at right), as well as the top-line Fury. Despite an impressive power-to-weight ratio, the Petty Engineering team of Lee and Richard Petty was one of the few to run 1961 Plymouths in NASCAR competition. When Lee was injured in one at the fourth race of the season at Daytona, Richard went on to take two wins and 18 top-five finishes during the season, though some of those races were run in a 1960 Plymouth.

Lee Petty's #42 Plymouth (foreground) ended up a little worse for the wear after a collision in a 100-mile preliminary race (inset) during the 1961 Daytona Speedweeks. Petty survived the incident and later returned to racing. In the background is son Richard's #43 Plymouth. Note that the NASCAR-mandated roll cage in Lee's car helped preserve the integrity of the cockpit, and that Lee was perched on what appears to be the stock Plymouth front seat.

1961
Pontiac

Pontiac hit its NASCAR stride in 1961, scoring a phenominal 30 wins in the season's 52 races. Yet despite its overwhelming success, Pontiac came in second to Chevrolet—with just 11 victories—for the Manufacturers Championship. On paper, the Pontiacs didn't appear as though they should have dominated the way they did. Fords probably weighed less and carried more power, at least if the numbers on their hoods were to be believed. (The make managed only seven wins despite an "advertised" 375 horsepower.) That's not to say the Pontiacs were underpowered,

however. New for '61 was a massive 421-cubic-inch V-8 that supplanted the 389 as the top engine. Pontiac hoods proclaimed it produced 368 hp, yet it probably produced more torque than the Ford's 390-cid engine, perhaps a nod to the old adage that "There's no substitute for cubic inches." Pontiacs carried fresh styling for 1961 but retained their trim-level names, moving up through the Catalina (what most NASCAR teams probably raced) to the Ventura shown at right, and on to the longer-wheelbase Star Chief and Bonneville.

Junior Johnson sits on the pole in his #27 Pontiac as the cars make a pace lap leading up to the Wilkes 200 at North Wilkesboro Speedway in North Carolina. Johnson finished fourth in the race and sixth in the season's points standings.

1962
Chevrolet

Full-size Chevrolets received a styling update for 1962 that included smoother flanks and loss of the V-shaped trim line between the taillights. As before, the low-line Biscayne and mid-line Bel Air (shown at right) had two taillamps on each side, while the top-line Impala had three—plus more brightwork. NASCAR teams logically used one of the "two-light" cars. The legendary 409-cubic-inch V-8 returned, now rated at up to 409 horsepower with "dual quads" (two four-barrel carbs), though NASCAR entries had to use a single-carb version with 380 hp. While Chevrolet had a good year with 14 victories, Pontiac cleaned house and took the Manufacturers Championship, with Chevy coming in second. As a "consolation prize," Chevrolet won the showroom sales race, moving a record two million units and trouncing second-place Ford by nearly 600,000.

Defending champion Ned Jarrett in the #11 Chevy is shown dueling with Joe Weatherly's #8 Pontiac. Although both cars were ostensibly sponsored by dealers—Jim Rathmann Chevrolet of Melbourne, Florida, and Gillman Pontiac in Houston, Texas—it was fairly well known in the racing community that these were merely "fronts" for factory support, which was still taboo under the 1957 AMA agreement.

1962
Pontiac

With the help of rising star Glen "Fireball" Roberts, Pontiac had another great NASCAR season in 1962. Although the company's win total dropped to "just" 22, that was enough to snare the Manufacturers Championship—what would prove to be both the first and the last for the brand. Pontiacs were treated to a facelift for '62 that didn't venture significantly from the '61 look. Yet Pontiac vaulted from fifth place to third in the sales race, a position it would hold through the end of the decade. Much of the brand's appeal during the era came from a growing performance reputation, something its success in NASCAR no doubt helped ignite. Pontiac's traditional full-size line was again divided into two wheelbases, the longer span carrying the Star Chief and top-line Bonneville. Returning on the shorter wheelbase was the Catalina, but replacing the Ventura was the "personal luxury" Grand Prix. The Catalina shown at right remained the best seller and also the car of choice for Pontiac's NASCAR efforts.

Fireball Roberts in the #22 Pontiac leads Richard Petty in the #43 Plymouth on the outside rail as they pass the #01 Ford of Billy Wade during the 1962 Daytona 500. Roberts went on to win the event, with Petty coming in second.

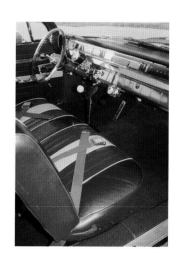

1963
Ford

Contrary to normal practice, Ford's 1963 NASCAR teams typically started with top-line Galaxie 500 models rather than low-line 300s. Why? Only the Galaxie 500 and 500XL pictured at right included the two-door "semi-fastback" Sports Hardtop that proved to be more aerodynamic at speed. These models also offered a bucket-seat interior and sport-themed trim. And the car wasn't just all show, as a four-speed manual transmission with floor shifter was available. Perhaps of most interest to racing teams, however, was 1963's newly optional 427-cubic-inch V-8 that put out up to 425 horsepower with dual four-barrel carburetors, though rules limited NASCAR teams to a 410-hp single-carb version. Fords racked up 23 victories for the season, edging out an up-and-coming Plymouth and flat-out walloping Pontiac and Chevy, the two former powerhouses scoring just four and eight wins, respectively. In the showroom, however, it was a different story, as Chevrolet again trounced Ford, this time by well over 600,000 units. Win some, lose some.

The Fords of #21 Tiny Lund (who was not at all tiny) and #11 Ned Jarrett battle it out in the late stages of the Daytona 500. Lund got his Ford ride when intended driver Marvin Panch was injured in an accident, and recommended that Lund —who had helped pull him from the wreckage—replace him. Lund had never won a NASCAR race in nine years of trying—until that day. Lund pulled off an upset victory in what became one of NASCAR's greatest stories.

1963
Plymouth

When Plymouth "downsized" its full-size models for 1962, the public responded with interest—interest in other makes, that is. Contrary to what Chrysler Corporation execs expected, car buyers maintained a "bigger is better" philosophy, which left the corporation high and dry with its smaller Dodges and Plymouths (Chryslers stayed about the same size). Somewhat odd styling didn't help, either. Plymouth forfeited its traditional third- or fourth-place slot in the sales rankings and slid all the way to eighth, an incredible drop. There was little the company could do to rebound for '63 besides clean up the styling a bit,

which it did, making it somewhat more conventional. Although probably not a big selling point to most buyers, Plymouth also bored out its existing 413-cubic-inch V-8 to 426 cid, providing up to 425 horsepower with dual four-barrel carburetors. In combination with the car's smaller size and lightweight "unibody" construction, these engines made Plymouths drag-strip terrors. They also made their mark in NASCAR competiton, though rules required a single four-barrel carburetor that trimmed horsepower somewhat. Plymouth racked up 19 victories in 1963, topped only by Ford's 23.

Sitting on the front row at the start of an event at the Bridgehampton Race Circuit in New York is Richard Petty's #43 Plymouth on the near side of Fred Lorenzen's Ford. Petty went on to take the win, one of 14 for the season and his first on a road course.

1964
Dodge

Dodge came out of a long NASCAR slump in 1964 to finish the season with 14 wins—second only to Ford's 30. Although that was two more than scored by sister-division Plymouth, Dodge placed behind its sibling in the final standings, ending the season in third. No small amount of both makes' success was undoubtedly due to the return of the Hemi engine, which had been discontinued after 1958. In its reincarnated form, the Hemi displaced 426 cubic inches and was rated at up to 425 horsepower—exactly the same as the previous wedgehead engine. However, that was with dual four-barrel carburetors,

and the engine was advertised as being "for off-road use only," though some found their way into street cars. Due to the carburetion setup, the 425-hp Hemi wasn't legal for NASCAR, so cars were fitted with a single four-barrel version, most proclaiming "400 H.P." on their hoods. But it quickly became clear that the Hemi's claimed horsepower figures were grossly underrated, especially after drivers such as Richard Petty qualified at Daytona at much higher speeds than they had in their '63 wedgehead cars. And it wasn't due to improved aerodynamics; the cars still carried a rather blocky profile, just as they had in '63.

Bobby Isaac in the #26 Dodge runs the high groove next to Jimmy Pardue in the #54 Plymouth. These two, along with Richard Petty in another Plymouth, raced to a photo finish in one of the 100-mile preliminary races at the Daytona Speedweeks. Although the official track camera malfunctioned, pictures taken by trackside photographers showed Isaac's Dodge crossed the finish line first.

1964
Mercury

Up to this time, Mercury had never made much of a splash in NASCAR, its best season being 1956 when the make took five wins—after which it began a long dry spell. It wasn't until 1963 that it scored another victory, and that led to five more in 1964. It was almost a mystery as to why the make did that well. Sure, it had a 427-cubic-inch V-8 making 410 horsepower on its side, but so did the lighter Fords—which won an astounding 30 races that year. Oddly, Mercury won four races in a row during July, all on either paved short tracks or road courses. The fifth win was also on a paved short track, so the Mercury's advantage didn't seem to be aerodynamics. It might have been preparation, however; all the winning Mercs came out of the Bud Moore shops, a famous organization in NASCAR circles. The make's model lineup started with the Monterey, then moved up to the Montclair (shown at right with optional rear fender skirts) and Park Lane, all on a 120-inch wheelbase. (Fords of the era were on a 119-inch span.) All full-size Mercurys came standard with a 390-cid V-8 making 250 to 330 hp, with the 427—in either 410-hp form or 425 with dual carburetors—being optional across the board.

Sophomore driver Billy Wade in the Bud Moore-prepared #1 Mercury runs in front of Paul Goldsmith (#25) and Richard Petty (#43) in the Southeastern 500 at Bristol Motor Speedway in Tennessee. Wade finished 10th in the event and a commendable fourth in the season's standings, scoring four of Mercury's five wins that year.

1964
Plymouth

Ever since Lee and Richard Petty began campaigning Plymouths in the late 1950s, the make had enjoyed a tremendous amount of NASCAR exposure and an impressive string of victories. The redesigned cars that arrived for 1964 continued that tradition, though they had newfound rivals in their own corporate cousins over at Dodge. Both makes benefited greatly from a revived Hemi V-8, now displacing 426 cubic inches and making up to 425 horsepower in the few examples that likely made it into street cars that year. But that dual-quad (two four-barrel carbure-

tors) version wasn't eligible for NASCAR, so Hemis for the track were advertised at 400 hp on most hoods, though Richard Petty's car carried a 405 figure. Both numbers were almost assuredly pessimistic, as the cars were significantly faster on the high-speed ovals than their predecessors—and their competitors. Plymouth racked up 12 wins during the 1964 season and was runner-up to Ford in the Manufacturers Championship. Showroom performance wasn't bad, either, as Plymouth sales jumped 22 percent.

Paul Goldsmith in the #25 Plymouth, Richard Petty in the #43 Plymouth, and Bobby Isaac in the #26 Dodge battle for the lead in the early stages of the Daytona 500. Petty emerged the winner, having lead 184 of the race's 200 laps, and went on to win the 1964 Drivers Championship.

1965

Ford

Although Ford recorded the highest winning percentage of any make in the history of NASCAR in 1965 (48 wins in 55 races or more than 87 percent), it was a rather hollow victory. When the Hemi engine used by Dodge and Plymouth factory teams was prohibited in NASCAR for 1965, the two companies pulled out in protest. Some independents still raced—and occasionally won—in the two makes, but Ford teams definitely had a huge advantage. Ford's full-size cars were completely redesigned that year with vertical headlights that probably didn't improve

aerodynamics. But it really didn't matter, at least in NASCAR. And the public seemed to embrace it, as Ford went from 1.6 million sales in 1964 to nearly 2.2 million for '65, just shy of Chevrolet's total. The full-size line contained only the Custom and the Galaxie 500 shown at right. The top engine offering was a 425-horsepower 427-cubic-inch V-8, a version of which was used in NASCAR. A change took place on the race cars this year, as the engine's cubic-inch displacement was shown on their hoods rather than the horsepower rating.

A lone Mercury flies with a flock of Fords in the early stages of the Daytona 500. The two makes took the top 13 spots in the race, all but two of them being Fords. Fred Lorenzen, running second in this photo in the #28 Ford, won the event, which was boycotted by the Dodge and Plymouth factory teams.

1966
Dodge Charger

NASCAR hit a stumbling block in the mid-1960s. When Dodges and Plymouths appeared at the tracks in 1964 with their new Hemi V-8s, Ford cried "Foul," insisting they weren't really "production" engines. Indeed, relatively few found their way into showroom-stock cars that year. As a result, the Hemi was outlawed for the 1965 season, and Dodge and Plymouth pulled out of NASCAR in protest. With Chevy and Pontiac already gone, that left Fords to battle it out with . . . other Fords. Not surprisingly, the make won 48 of 55 races that year, and fans didn't take well to the lack of competition. As more Hemis were built and made more readily available in street cars, NASCAR reversed its decision and allowed them to run in 1966. Coinciding with that was the introduction of Dodge's sleek new Charger. Essentially a Dodge Coronet with an aerodynamic fastback roofline, the car seemed tailor-made for racing. Dodge won 18 events in 1966—more than any other make—but not all were with Chargers. The car featured a hidden-headlight grille, full-width taillights, a four-bucket-seat interior, center console, and folding rear seatbacks. A 318-cubic-inch V-8 was standard, but the mighty 425-horsepower 426 Hemi was optional.

David Pearson in the #6 Dodge Charger leads Cale Yarborough in the #27 Ford, Richard Petty in the #43 Plymouth, and Paul Goldsmith in the #99 Plymouth during the Daytona 500. Pearson finished third behind winner Petty and second-place Yarborough.

1967
Ford Fairlane

When Dodge and Plymouth elected to race intermediate-size cars after their full-sizers went back to truly being full-size, some Ford teams responded by using the company's intermediate-size Fairlane (shown at right), which rode a 116-inch wheelbase compared to the 119-inch span of the company's full-size models. Sibling Mercury did the same, but didn't share in Ford's success; whereas Ford won 10 races and the Manufacturers Championship, Mercury won zero races and placed fifth out of five makes. Spurred by the mid-'60s success of the Pontiac GTO—which launched the "muscle-car era" by carrying Pontiac's biggest V-8 in an intermediate-size body—Fairlanes now offered a wide range of engines, from a pedestrian 200-cubic-inch six to potent 390- and 427-cid V-8s, the latter producing up to 425 horsepower. The Fairlane 500 pictured at right carries a 320-hp 390-cid V-8, making it a potent street performer.

Formula One champion Jimmy Clark made just one NASCAR start in his career, and this was it: the 1967 American 500 held at North Carolina Speedway in Rockingham, North Carolina. Although fellow Ford driver Bobby Allison won the race, Clark didn't fare as well, blowing the engine of his #66 Ford Fairlane after just 144 laps of the 500-lap event.

1967
Plymouth Belvedere

Plymouth had been a strong NASCAR contender throughout the 1960s, but the company really hit its stride in 1967. With a Hemi engine under the hood and Richard Petty behind the wheel, Plymouths won 31 of 49 races that year, 27 going to Petty, who handily won the Drivers Championship. Oddly, Plymouth somehow came in second for the Manufacturers Championship to Ford, which scored 10 victories. A notable rule change for 1967 would eventually have far-reaching consequences. For the first time, teams were allowed to reinforce or alter a car's frame for safety. This mostly affected the unibody Dodges and Plymouths, as it allowed them to run specially built frames as long as the stock body dimensions were kept. Although the full-size Plymouths returned to typical full-size dimensions for 1965 after their 1962 downsizing, most NASCAR teams raced the intermediate-sized Belvedere, represented by the high-performance GTX shown at right. These sat on the same 116-inch wheelbase as the downsized full-size cars of 1962-64. Showroom engine choices ranged from a lowly 225-cubic-inch "slant six" to potent 383- and 440-cid V-8s and culminated with the fire-breathing 426 Hemi.

Richard Petty in the #43 Plymouth nudges Darel Dieringer's Ford as they charge into the first turn on the opening lap of the Virginia 500 at Martinsville Speedway. As was the case in so many races in 1967, Petty ended up taking the win.

1968
Dodge Charger

While 1968 wasn't a great year for Dodge on the NASCAR tracks, it was a stunning year for the make in showroom sales. Part of that success stemmed from a redesigned Charger featuring an envelope body with buttressed fastback roofline, distinct round taillights, and a full-width sunken grille hosting hidden headlights. But what looked sleek on the street really didn't cut the air all that well on the track, so the Charger wasn't the runaway winner it looked to be. Still, Dodge amassed five victories during the season, most at the hands of Bobby Isaacs, runner-up in the points race to David Pearson. Chargers were offered in base and sportier R/T trim levels with a wide range of engines, from the mild 225-cubic-inch slant six, through a host of V-8s, all the way up to the wild 425-horsepower 426-cubic-inch Hemi. (The R/T at right carries the popular 330-hp 383 V-8.) Sales of more than 96,000 exceeded the impressive total of the original Charger by better than 250 percent, making the 1968 version a stunning success—at least as far as dealers were concerned.

The #6 Dodge Charger of Charlie Glotzbach shares the front row with LeeRoy Yarbrough's Ford at the start of the Volunteer 500 at Bristol Motor Speedway in Tennessee. Glotzbach ran with the leaders until his engine blew, a common failing on this hot July day. In fact, only 13 of the 36 starters finished the race. David Pearson, shown here on the outside of the third row, emerged victorious.

1968

Plymouth Road Runner

Plymouth redesigned its midsize line for 1968, offering it in five models with a wide range of engines. Belvedere was the base trim level, followed by the Satellite, Sport Satellite, new-for-'68 Road Runner, and top-line GTX. Without a doubt, it was the Road Runner that caused the biggest stir on the street. While Pontiac's GTO is usually lauded as the first "muscle car," the Road Runner broke ground as the first budget muscle car. Essentially a stripped-down Belvedere with the GTX's louvered hood covering a standard 335-horsepower 383-cubic-inch V-8, the Road Runner started at just $2896. By contrast, a

GTO tipped the price scale at $3101—and it didn't offer the Road Runner's cartoon graphics or soon-to-be-famous "beep-beep" horn. Road Runner was available as a two-door coupe or more-expensive two-door hardtop, and offered the fabled 425-hp 426 Hemi as an option—at a stiff $714. In one of the worst sales forecasts ever, Plymouth anticipated selling about 2500 units . . . and sold nearly 45,000. Only 1019 got the Hemi fitted to the coupe at right. On the track, Plymouth once again owed much of its racing success to Richard Petty, who single-handedly accounted for all of the make's 16 NASCAR victories.

Richard Petty in the #43 Plymouth leads the pace lap of the Hillsborough 150 at Orange Speedway in Hillsborough, North Carolina. In what proved to be the last NASCAR race at the 0.9-mile dirt oval, Petty won the event with a seven-lap lead over runner-up James Hylton.

1969
Dodge Charger Daytona

After Ford trotted out the aerodynamic Torino Talladega that dominated 1969's early season Daytona 500, Dodge made a concerted effort to catch up. First came the Charger 500 with a flush-mounted rear window and flush-mounted grille, but that wasn't enough to do the trick. Then the company pulled out all the stops, introducing one of the most bizarre creations ever to hit the track … or the street. Taking the Talladega's sloped nose to—quite literally—greater lengths, Dodge grafted an 18-inch pointed beak and towering rear spoiler onto the Charger 500 and named it after the premier track on the NASCAR circuit. The Dodge Daytona made its debut at that year's Talladega 500 in September and took the checkered flag, resulting in the rather odd irony that the Talladega won at Daytona and the Daytona won at Talladega. Dodge built about 505 "street" versions of the Daytona to qualify it for NASCAR competition. Standard was a 375-horsepower 440-cubic-inch V-8. The 426 Hemi was an option chosen by only 70 buyers, one of them being the original owner of the car at right. Whereas a standard Charger V-8 could be had for as little as $3126, the Daytona started at $4000—a bargain considering its eventual "collector" value.

The inaugural Talladega 500 at the newly opened Talladega Superspeedway made an instant star out of little-known Richard Brickhouse. Substituting for Charlie Glotzbach in the #99 Dodge Daytona, he out-dueled fellow Dodge drivers Bobby Isaac (#71) and Jim Vandiver (#3) to score an upset victory,

1969
Ford Torino Talladega

As speeds on the tracks rose higher and higher, aerodynamics became more and more important. Ford's sleek fastback Torino of 1968 proved to be a lethal NASCAR weapon, helping the company to 21 victories and the Manufacturers Championship. But Ford didn't rest on its laurels. For the 1969 season, an even slipperier warrior was sent into battle, this version named after the new high-speed, high-banked Talladega Superspeedway. Changes to the Torino Talladega's body were subtle, but they made a measurable aerodynamic difference at speed. Most notable was an elongated, angled nose that sheered off the right-angle edge formed by the hood and grille. Since NASCAR rules mandated that a certain number of examples be made available to the public in order to qualify as "stock cars," Ford built 754 Talladegas for street use. While competition versions typically carried a 427- or 429-cubic-inch V-8, civilian models came with a 428 Cobra Jet engine rated at 335 horsepower and were fitted with an automatic transmission. All were produced in early 1969 in order to qualify the car for the February 23 Daytona 500, which was won by LeeRoy Yarbrough in a Talladega.

LeeRoy Yarbrough in the #98 Torino Talladega battles Buddy Baker's Dodge in the Wilkes 400 at North Wilkesboro Speedway. At .625 mile, the Wilkesboro track was hardly the type of superspeedway for which the Talladega was designed. Yet the cars took three of the top four positions in the race, with Yarbrough finishing fourth behind winner David Pearson, also in a Talladega.

1970
Plymouth Superbird

Similar to what sister-division Dodge had done with its Charger Daytona in 1969, Plymouth added a pointy snout and tall rear wing to its Road Runner for 1970 and called it the "Superbird." With a car that was now competitive on the high-speed tracks, Plymouth lured Richard Petty back after his one-year stint with Ford. That, perhaps as much as any changes to the car itself, helped Plymouth amass 21 victories in 1970, the most of any make. It still came in second in the standings to Dodge, however, which continued to run its Daytona on the high-banked ovals and scored 17 wins. Against Chrysler Corporation's aero assault, Ford and Mercury combined could muster only 10 victories. To qualify the Superbird for NASCAR competition, Plymouth built 1920 "street" versions, all fitted with black vinyl tops and black panels over the headlights. Engine choices included the standard 375-horsepower 440-cubic-inch V-8, a version with three two-barrel carbs and 390 hp known as the "440 Six Pack," and the 425-hp 426 Hemi. Prices started at a lofty $4298, a whopping $1400 more than a base Road Runner, but an absolute steal in today's light.

Richard Petty was "back home" in his traditional #43 Plymouth for the 1970 season after spending a year on the Ford team. He's shown passing the grandstands at North Carolina Motor Speedway in Rockingham, North Carolina, during the Carolina 500—which he won.

1971
Chevrolet Monte Carlo

Chevrolet hadn't enjoyed a strong presence in NASCAR since the factory dropped its support in the early '60s, but the make came roaring back in the early '70s. Much of that was due not to Chevrolet, but to Charlotte Motor Speedway manager Richard Howard. Thinking a Chevy in the starting field might lure more fans to his track, Howard formed a team with former driver Junior Johnson as manager and Charlie Glotzbach behind the wheel. Their car of choice was a Chevrolet Monte Carlo, which had been introduced for 1970 as a "personal luxury" car to compete in the marketplace (though not on the track) with Ford's

Thunderbird. Howard and his team won only one race in 1971, but added driver Bobby Allison—and a lot more wins—the following year. The Monte Carlo offered to the public sat on the same 116-inch wheelbase as the midsize Chevelle sedan but came only as a two-door coupe with long-hood/short-deck proportions. It came with a 245-horsepower 350-cubic-inch V-8, but the SS (Super Sport) version shown at right featured a 454-cid V-8 with 365 horsepower standard, up to 425 as an option. First-generation Monte Carlos raced alongside their Chevelle siblings early in the decade and were redesigned for 1973.

Bobby Allison in his #12 Monte Carlo duels with Richard Petty going into the final lap of a 1972 race at North Wilkesboro Speedway. The two drivers had slugged it out toward the end, both of their cars being battered in the process; Allison's was smoking so badly he could hardly see out. Petty passed Allison during the final lap after both cars hit the wall, resulting in one of the most thrilling finishes in NASCAR history.

1971
Mercury Cyclone Spoiler

It wasn't the droop-snoot aerodynamic wonder of its 1969 namesake (which shared its styling with the Ford Torino Talladega), but the redesigned Mercury Cyclone Spoiler that appeared on NASCAR tracks in the early '70s still made its mark on the history books. During the 1971 season, Mercury teams could continue to run their 1969 Spoilers, but starting in 1972, NASCAR rules forced them to upgrade to a newer model. Many only took two steps forward and raced 1971 Cyclone Spoilers, perhaps fearing the restyled 1972 midsize Mercury (which now came only as the Montego, as the performance-oriented Cyclone version didn't return) wouldn't be as slippery on the high-speed tracks. Whether true or not, the '71 Cyclone Spoiler continued its predecessor's success, winning nine races in 1972—second only to Chevy's 10. Versions sold to the public came standard with a 351-cubic-inch V-8, with the option of a 429 with up to 375 horsepower. But "performance" was becoming an increasingly dirty word, and sales of the Cyclone—which had topped 13,000 in 1970—dwindled to just 3084 for '71. Only 353 of those were the top-line Spoiler edition shown at right, making it a rare example of Mercury's last muscle-car breath.

The #21 Mercury of David Pearson rounds a turn at Martinsville Speedway during the 1972 Virginia 500. Pearson dropped out of this race with a blown transmission, but he and his Mercury managed an impressive six wins in only 17 starts during the 31-race 1972 season.

1971
Plymouth Road Runner

Plymouth redesigned its midsize line for 1971 with "fuselage" styling incorporating a high beltline flowing over raised rear fenders. A dumbell-shaped front bumper surrounded a recessed grille, and the rear window was notched, neither of which likely helped the car's aerodynamics on the high-speed NASCAR tracks. But that didn't seem to matter. Plymouths won 22 races in 1971—10 more than runner-up Mercury— along with the Manufacturers Championship, the first ever for the Plymouth brand ... and also, as it turned out, the last. As usual, most of the credit went to Richard Petty, who accounted for all but one of Plymouth's wins and earned himself his third Drivers Championship. Things were also looking up in the showroom, as Plymouth jumped from fourth to third in the sales race. The new midsize line was trimmed from five models to just one: the carried-over Satellite, of which the Road Runner pictured at right was a sub-series. Lower compression ratios mandated by a requirement that cars be able to run on unleaded fuel meant many engines lost some power, but the 'Runner's top 426 Hemi found in the featured example was still rated at 425 horses. The less-costly 440 Six-Pack (badged "440+6") option was likewise unaffected, retaining its 390-hp claim, but the standard 383 dropped from 335 hp to 300. Added for 1971 was a "downsize" option, a 275-hp 340 V-8. But the age of the muscle car was coming to a close, and despite its attributes—and NASCAR success—this marked the beginning of the end for the "beep-beep" bird.

Richard Petty takes the high groove in his #43 Plymouth as he runs neck-and-neck with Charlie Glotzbach's #3 Chevy during the Firecracker 400 at Daytona. Petty finished second behind Bobby Isaac.

1972
AMC Matador

American Motors Corporation was the outgrowth of a 1954 merger between Hudson and Nash, and was best known for the economy-oriented Rambler model that evolved into its own nameplate. In the late '60s, "Rambler" gave way to "AMC," possibly because the company wanted to shed its economy image in the wake of some planned sporty models and the acquisition of Jeep. Perhaps spurred by that intent, the company jumped into racing and fielded (to many people's surprise) a NASCAR team. Bound for the track was the company's midsize Matador, a name born in 1971 to replace "Rebel." The cars looked

nice enough and generally undercut Big Three rivals in price, but the Matador never became a hot seller. It did make its mark on the track, however. Road racer Mark Donahue drove a factory-backed Matador to some decent finishes in 1972 and a surprise victory at the Riverside road course in '73. Street versions typically sported lowly six-cylinder engines or modest V-8s, but the top engine option was a stomping 401-cubic-inch V-8 rated at 255 horsepower under the new-for-'72 "net" rating system. With that powerhouse under the hood, a Matador wasn't a car you could bully around.

Mark Donahue wheels the #16 Matador to a win at the Riverside road course in 1973. It marked AMC's first NASCAR victory and the only one that year. AMC continued to race 1972 versions of the Matador in 1973 but replaced it with a redesigned car in '74.

1972
Dodge Charger

Dodge redesigned its Charger for 1971, giving it a wedge-shaped profile and semi-fastback roofline. On NASCAR tracks, it followed on the heels of the wildly successful Daytona, giving it awfully big shoes to fill. Although they shared their basic shape with the contemporary Plymouth Road Runners, Chargers didn't benefit from the expertise of Plymouth's factory-backed Richard Petty team. As a result, Dodge scored seven wins in '71 vs. Plymouth's 22. But Petty moved over to Dodge in 1973, and the make's fortunes improved. In all, this generation of Charger won 56 races—and brought Petty two championships—

through 1977, after which it was replaced in NASCAR competition by the hapless Magnum. Street versions, however, didn't last that long, being supplanted for '75 by a redesigned version with a boxier silhouette. The 1972 model shown at right represents the third-generation Charger in its original form with upswept side-window treatment. With the famous Hemi being retired after '71, the Rallye version pictured carried the biggest engine offered, a 440-cubic-inch V-8 advertised at 330 horsepower under the new "net" rating system—enough to let the Charger live up to its name.

The #71 Dodge Charger of Buddy Baker qualified on the pole for the 1973 running of the Winston 500 at Talladega. Baker was leading the race when he became involved in a 21-car accident. David Pearson, shown beside Baker in this shot, avoided the collision and went on to win.

1973
Chevrolet Chevelle

Chevrolet's midsize cars were redesigned for 1973 with smooth "Colonnade" styling, and it wasn't long before they found their way onto the tracks. Convertibles and pillarless hardtops were gone, and the flowing silhouette of the new Chevelle was a complete departure from that of the previous generation. Federal requirements mandated that all 1973 cars be fitted with five-mph front bumpers, and the Chevelle wore its "girder" better than most. Though performance was being downplayed and performance-oriented cars were on the wane by this time, the Chevelle lineup included the SS version shown at right

with sporty trim and an available 454-cubic-inch V-8 rated at 245 net horsepower. An interesting option was swivel bucket seats, an idea taken from Chryslers of the late '50s that eased entry and exit. Several NASCAR drivers raced the new Chevelles through the mid-'70s, including Cale Yarborough and brothers Donnie and Bobby Allison. Oddly, other teams favored Chevy's personal-luxury Monte Carlo, also redesigned for 1973, and the siblings often battled each other on the track. Together they accounted for 19 total wins in 1973 and '74 and gave Chevrolet the Manufacturers Championship both years.

Cale Yarborough in the #11 Chevy battles Richard Petty in the final laps of the National 500 at Charlotte Motor Speedway. Yarborough passed Petty 22 laps from the finish and led the rest of the way. During the postrace inspection, "disturbing" engine readings indicated both cars may have been running oversized engines, but the drivers were allowed to keep their 1-2 finishes, and no penalties were assessed.

1975
AMC Matador

As the Rambler nameplate was being phased out in favor of AMC badges in the mid-1960s, the company ventured from its traditional conservative path. First came the swoopy, fastback Marlin, followed by the sporty Javelin "ponycar" and its truncated, two-seat brother, the AMX. Flamboyantly colorful performance versions of the lowly American (the Scrambler) and stodgy Matador (The Machine) capitalized on the muscle-car mania then sweeping the country, and the stubby Gremlin that followed for 1970 went after the import market. The trend subsided after the 1975 introduction of the odd little Pacer ("The first wide small car"), but just before that came a redesigned Matador coupe with thoroughly distinctive—and somewhat polarizing—styling. AMC already had a NASCAR program in place, and the team switched to the new Matador for the 1974-75 seasons, after which AMC pulled the plug. But Matadors won four races during this period, a commendable performance. Street versions were available with the Sporty "X" package that brought side stripes and fancy wheels. Engine compartments could hold a 235-horsepower 401-cubic-inch V-8 in '74, up to a 175-hp 360 in the '75 Matador X shown at right.

Bobby Allison's Matador snakes its way through the "esses" on Riverside's road course on the way to victory in the season-opening Winston Western 500. Allison led all but 18 of the 191 laps.

1976
Chevrolet Monte Carlo

Along with its midsize stablemate, the Chevelle, Chevrolet's personal-luxury Monte Carlo was redesigned for 1973. Also like the Chevelle, it was raced. This generation was built only through 1977—after which it was downsized significantly—but NASCAR rules allowed the "big" cars on the tracks until after the first event of 1981. During its five-year production span, the Monte Carlo saw few changes, the biggest being the addition of the federally required five-mph rear bumper in 1974 (to join the one required in front from '73), and a switch from single round headlights to stacked rectangular lights for '76. As with many cars of the period, horsepower suffered as the years progressed. While all Monte Carlos of this generation came standard with a V-8, the top engine was originally a 270-hp 454-cubic-inch big-block. It was down to 235 hp by 1975, the final year it was offered in the Monte Carlo. The biggest engine for '76 was a 175-hp 400, and for swan-song '77, a 170-horse 350. Chevrolet had a strong winning streak going during this Monte Carlo's tenure, racking up more than 100 victories and seven Manufacturers Championships.

Richard Petty's #43 Monte Carlo runs inches ahead of Darrell Waltrip's #88 Monte in a legendary duel on the banks of Darlington Raceway in the 1979 running of the Rebel 500. The pair swapped the lead seven times in the last five laps, with Waltrip finally edging out Petty for the win.

1977
Oldsmobile Cutlass

Not only was the 1973-77 Cutlass one of the best-selling cars of the '70s, but it also brought Oldsmobile back into NASCAR competition—and the winner's circle. Like all midsize GM cars, the '73 Cutlass wore "Colonnade" styling that was striking for its time and helped give Oldsmobile a string of third-place finishes in the showroom sales race behind Chevrolet and Ford. Sculpted sides gave way to smoother flanks on coupes for 1976, when a beveled nose also became available on some models—neither of which hurt the car's chances on the track. Few changes marked the 1977 models, the last example of this generation of

Cutlasses; after that, the car was significantly down-sized. The odd thing is that the Colonnade generation made its biggest splash in NASCAR competition after the car itself had already been discontinued. Several drivers raced 1977 Cutlasses in '78, including Cale Yarborough, who garnered 10 of Oldsmobile's 12 wins—the first for the brand since 1959—along with his third consecutive NASCAR championship. By that time, street versions had lost a bit of their performance edge, but the famed 4-4-2 shown at right was still available with a potent-for-the-day 185-horsepower 403-cubic-inch V-8.

Cale Yarborough in the #11 Oldsmobile leads a trio of contenders in the NAPA National 500 at Charlotte Motor Speedway in 1978 on the way to his third consecutive NASCAR championship. Yarborough blew his engine during the race, but his crew installed a new one in just 13 minutes, and he went on to a 22nd-place finish.

1981
Ford Thunderbird

As was the case with many American cars of the era, Ford significantly downsized its personal-luxury Thunderbird after the second oil crisis in 1979. The new model appeared for 1980 nearly six inches shorter in wheelbase and about 800 pounds lighter than its predecessor. It boasted very boxy, "formal" styling, hardly the ticket for high-speed NASCAR tracks. Yet the car fared quite well after being introduced to the circuit in 1981, netting Ford nine wins in the two years it was active in racing. Despite this success, however, the car wasn't a strong seller. The previous generation, introduced for 1977, had itself been downsized

significantly and enjoyed sales that peaked at more than 350,000 in 1978. But the version introduced for 1980 barely managed 150,000 units in its debut year and went downhill from there before being replaced by a more "aero" design for 1983. The 1980-82 T-Birds were the first to offer a six-cylinder engine—two, actually, the first being a 200-cubic-inch straight six, the latter a 232-cid V-6. V-8s were still available, but they were downsized as well. Offered for 1981 was a 130-hp 302, while the top engine for swan-song 1982 was a 120-hp 255. The T-Bird was still flying, but its once-mighty wings had been clipped.

Bill Elliott qualified on the pole in his #9 Thunderbird for the CRC Chemicals 500 at Darlington. At the time, Elliott was a small-time independent running with limited sponsorship funds, yet he managed an impressive fourth-place finish in the race.

1981
Pontiac Grand Prix

It had been a long time since Pontiac had enjoyed much NASCAR exposure when the make won its first race in 18 years during the 1981 season. Although the midsize LeMans was also used, most Pontiac teams raced the rather boxy-looking Grand Prix, long known more for luxury than sport. Through the end of this design generation in 1987, Pontiac amassed a total of 13 wins—not a bad showing after such a long dry spell. Like its corporate siblings over at Buick, Chevrolet, and Oldsmobile, the Grand Prix had undergone a severe downsizing for the 1978 model year, adopt-

ing a body style that would be used for a decade. Though less festooned than many cars of the era, the 1981 Grand Prix still offered such period touches as opera windows, half-vinyl landau roof, wire wheels, woodgrain trim, velour upholstery, and stand-up hood ornament as seen on the LJ model shown at right. Under the hood were other signs of the times: The standard 110-horsepower 231-cubic-inch V-6 could be replaced by a 120-horsepower 265-cubic-inch V-8, or a 105-hp 350-cid *diesel* V-8.

Although Dale Earnhardt and the number "3" have since become almost synonymous, the first time he raced a car with that number was midway through the 1981 season—after he'd already won his first championship. The car was a Grand Prix fielded by the Richard Childress team and sponsored by Wrangler, which had been Earnhardt's sponsor at another team where he started the year in the #2 Grand Prix, shown trailing with Joe Ruttman at the wheel.

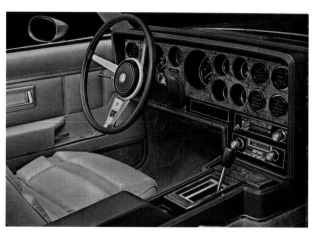

1982
Buick Regal

Not since 1955 had a Buick visited NASCAR's Victory Lane when, in 1981, a Regal took the checkered flag—followed later that year by 21 more. Buick came out of nowhere to be the dominant force in NASCAR racing during the 1981 and '82 seasons, winning a stunning 47 of 61 events. A number of top-flight drivers piloted Buicks during this time period, including Darrell Waltrip, Cale Yarborough, and "The King," Richard Petty, who drove a Buick to victory in the 1981 Daytona 500. Bobby Allison switched to Buicks in 1982 and was rewarded with a Daytona 500 win of his own. A 1981 reskin brought a chiseled look that made this generation of Regals particularly appealing and was augmented by some decidedly un-Buick-like performance models that were some of the hottest cars of their era. Although the first Regal Grand National of 1982 (shown at right) was a limited-production styling exercise with a fairly mild 4.1-liter V-6 beneath its flashy exterior, later versions were known for their brutish turbocharged 3.8-liter V-6s. This engine, initially rated at 150-165 horsepower when introduced for 1978, would be boosted to 245 hp in later models, and as much as 276 hp in the limited-edition 1987 GNX. All are valuable collectibles today.

Terry Labonte keeps his #44 Buick Regal just ahead of #27 Cale Yarborough and #88 Bobby Allison in the Gabriel 400 at Michigan International Speedway. Labonte blew his engine later in the race, while Yarborough went on to take the victory.

1983
Chevrolet Monte Carlo SS

A surprising performance revival was taking place in the early 1980s as manufacturers began coming to grips with the emissions standards that strangled engines of the mid- to late-'70s. One of the earliest examples of what would become known as "modern muscle cars" appeared for 1983 courtesy of the folks from Chevrolet. The fabled "SS" moniker returned to grace a sporty version of the personal-luxury Monte Carlo, bringing with it a swoopy new nose, sporty interior and exterior trim, and a 175-horsepower 305-cubic-inch V-8. The Monte Carlo SS became a legend on both street and track. Its smooth front fascia gave it an aerodynamic advantage at high speeds that helped Chevrolet boost its NASCAR victory total from just three in 1982 to 15 in '83, netting it the first of what would become a long string of Manufacturers Championships.

Neil Bonnett in the #75 Chevy Monte Carlo SS leads a pack of challengers in the 1983 running of the Warner W. Hodgdon Carolina 500 at North Carolina Motor Speedway. Bonnett qualified second, but his luck didn't hold, as the rear end of his car went out just nine laps from the finish.

1983

Ford Thunderbird

After some rather lackluster NASCAR seasons in the '70s and early '80s, Ford battled back in the mid-'80s with a sleek new Thunderbird seemingly tailor-made for the tracks. Contrary to its boxy predecessor, the redesigned T-Bird introduced for 1983 had curves where there used to be edges, all the better for airflow over the body at high speeds. Whether the stylists had racing or merely showroom sales in mind, their design succeeded in both venues. This generation of T-Bird lasted through 1986, during which time NASCAR wins jumped by 60 percent over the previous four-year span and sales compared to

the previous "boxy 'Bird" went up nearly the same amount. One change in strategy for 1983 was a version with sporty overtones: the Turbo Coupe. While the reinstituted 302-cubic-inch V-8 put out 140 horsepower, the Turbo Coupe held a 140-cid turbo four yielding 142 hp, and it could even be paired with a manual transmission—the first offered in a T-Bird in a very long time. While never particularly popular with buyers, the little turbo four remained the top power option throughout the model's tenure and continued to be so into the next generation.

The first of what would be many NASCAR victories for Bill Elliott came during the 1983 season finale at Riverside. Elliott drove Harry Melling's #9 Thunderbird, a combination that would eventually bring the team a championship—and a few NASCAR records.

1986
Chevrolet Monte Carlo SS Aerocoupe

After Ford's sleek new Thunderbird challenged Chevrolet's NASCAR dominance in 1985 (each make winning 14 races), the Bow Tie Boys fielded an aero-influenced version of the Monte Carlo SS to take back what the wind had taken away. Since NASCAR rules still mandated that bodies match those of at least a limited number of production vehicles, Chevrolet released 200 copies of what was called the Monte Carlo SS Aerocoupe for 1986. The biggest change was a sloped, compound-curve backlight and correspondingly shorter trunklid. To many eyes, it didn't do the overall look any favors, but Chevy said it dropped the drag coefficient of the standard SS (black car at right) from 0.38 to 0.365, a noteworthy benefit on the high-speed ovals. In other ways, the two versions were essentially identical. Chevy built 6052 more Aerocoupes for 1987, but the model didn't return for '88, the rear-drive Monte's swan-song year. All Aerocoupes were powered by a 180-horsepower 305-cubic-inch V-8 and four-speed automatic transmission, same as the regular SS. Chevrolet ran the Aerocoupe in NASCAR through the first few races of the 1989 season. After that, it was replaced by rear-wheel-drive racing versions of Chevy's new front-wheel-drive Lumina coupe.

A pair of Monte Carlo SS Aerocoupes battle side-by-side during the Oakwood Homes 500 at Charlotte Motor Speedway. Dale Earnhardt in the #3 Chevy lapped Tim Richmond in the #25 Chevy—along with nearly everyone else—to take the win. It was one of five victories scored by Earnhardt in 1986 on the way to his second championship.

1986
Pontiac Grand Prix 2+2

Pontiac's taste of racing success in the mid-1980s after a decades-long dry spell seemed to whet the company's appetite for victory on NASCAR's high-speed ovals. When Ford suddenly started winning with its newly minted "Aero 'Bird," Pontiac responded with a sleeker version of its race track warrior. Arriving for 1986 as the Grand Prix 2+2, it carried a "bubble-back" rear window to smooth out the airflow—and thus reduce the drag—over the squared-off roofline of the "regular" Grand Prix. It also got a smoother front end courtesy of a unique urethane snout bearing a twin-nostril grille. The strategy worked, as Ponti-

acs promptly returned to the winner's circle. Although the number is in question, it's thought that only about 200 2+2s were built for 1986, and it doesn't appear they returned for '87. All were fitted with the same 180-horsepower 305-cubic-inch V-8 used in the similarly themed Chevrolet Monte Carlo SS Aerocoupe. However, the SS Aerocoupe shared its grille with the normal Monte Carlo SS, making it less distinctive. Furthermore, Chevrolet built 6252 Aerocoupes over two years, meaning the Pontiac 2+2 is an unusually rare collectible today.

Richard Petty in the #43 Pontiac duels with fellow NASCAR legend Dale Earnhardt in the Wrangler Jeans Indigo 400 at Richmond International Raceway. The pair finished fourth and second, respectively, behind winner Tim Richmond.

1987
Ford Thunderbird

After the "Aero 'Bird" of 1983 experienced a fair degree of success on the NASCAR tracks, Ford brought out an even sleeker T-Bird for 1987. While the silhouette was nearly identical, the headlights were now flush-mounted, and the returning Turbo Coupe featured a unique grilleless nose. Engine offerings were little changed: A 120-horsepower 3.8-liter V-6 was still standard, with a 150-hp 302 V-8 optional. The Turbo Coupe returned with its 2.3-liter turbocharged four, now rated at 190 hp. Perhaps because the new design looked very similar to the old and there wasn't much that was newsworthy under the hood, the car

didn't do that well in the showroom. But it fared very well on the tracks. Besides taking 11 wins for 1987 and another nine in '88—the only two years this design was run—this T-Bird has the distinction of holding the all-time NASCAR qualifying record. It was achieved in 1987 by Bill Elliott, who first set the record at Daytona with a 210.364-mph run, then broke it later that year at Talladega by turning in a 212.809-mph perfor- mance. Amid concerns over ever-increasing speeds, NASCAR quickly made rules changes that have since kept qualifying speeds below 200 mph, thus cement- ing Elliott's—and the T-Bird's—place in history.

Bill Elliott kneels next to the #9 Thunderbird that put him in the record books—prob- ably to stay. He first set the lap-speed qualify- ing record at 210.364 mph in February 1987 at Daytona (where this photo was taken), then promptly broke it in April at Talladega with a 212.809-mph run. Shortly thereafter, NASCAR made rules changes in order to keep qualifying speeds below 200 mph, meaning Elliott's marks will likely never be broken.